INDIAN TRADE GOODS

ARTHUR WOODWARD

OREGON ARCHAEOLOGICAL SOCIETY

ISBN: 0-8323-0136-1

First Edition 1965

Second Edition 1976

Second Printing 1989

Binford & Mort Publishing
Portland, Oregon

INTRODUCTION

The manuscript for "Indian Trade Goods" was originally submitted by Mr. Woodward in 1959 and ran serially in "Screenings", the monthly publication of the Oregon Archaeological Society. The article proved to be very popular and extra copies of "Screenings" containing the series were soon exhausted. In response to popular demand the Society decided to publish the article in this more convenient form with the permission of the author. Mr. Woodward has been associated with the Los Angeles County Museum and several other organizations, and is at present with the University of Arizona. He is a nationally known authority on Indian trade goods.

The publication of this pamphlet affords an opportunity to include some supplemental data, which are contained in the Appendix. Dr. T. N. Campbell, editor of "American Antiquity", kindly granted permission to reproduce Mr. Olsen's discussion on buttons which of all trade goods are the easiest to classify and date, with the possible exception of guns.

The illustrations in this pamphlet are by the editor, who assumes full responsibility for the titles and data accompanying them. The Oregon Archaeological Society hopes that this publication will supplement the meager literature on Indian trade goods, and will stimulate further research on this fascinating subject.

Emory Strong, editor

INDIAN TRADE GOODS

by

Arthur Woodward

The use of the term "trade goods" in relation to those objects of European origin which found their way into the hands of the Indians on the North American continent from the 16th century through the 19th is, in a sense, a misnomer. Under this category collectors, archaeologists, historians and ethnologists have lumped all items either traded, sold or given outright to the tribesman. In certain areas as many gifts were made of blankets, guns, beads, paint, weapons of the edged variety, kettles, agricultural implements, textiles, bottles, buttons, ornaments, etc., by the French, British, Dutch, Spanish and American governments as were exchanged by individuals for profit.

However, since the terminology seems fixed, there is no logical reason for discriminating in either the types or methods of the distribution of these goods. Hence in the following article the term "trade goods" may be understood to mean all classifications, official and unofficial, of the hundreds of articles given or traded to the Indians.

The varieties of these goods increased during the four centuries of contact and according to the likes and dislikes of the recipients. Thus in the beginning the items given in trade were relatively few and the quality and diversity of them were governed by the whims of the distributors. Both sides learned rapidly. The Europeans, at the outset, were inclined to look upon the Indians as fabulous beings and the gifts which were showered upon the tribesmen were in some cases quite valuable. But, as the contacts became more common, the "naked savage" idea prevailed and anything was deemed good enough.

The natives on the other hand first looked upon the white strangers as people of great wealth and were welcomed. The few beads, axes, knives, kettles and pieces of cloth were received as avidly as were expensive Venetian goblets, cloth-of-gold, and fine clothes. It was when the Indians learned that these newcomers were only human like themselves and that they valued the furs of the animals which roamed the forest, the mountain and the sea more than they did the objects of metal and cloth, and the glittering baubles of brass, silver and glass, that the aborigines began to strike harder bargains.

The natives of the various parts of the country lived differently, ate different foods, hunted different animals and reacted in a different manner to the trade goods brought to them by the white men. Thus when the Spanish conquistadores first encountered the Indians on the east coast of Mexico not far from Vera Cruz in 1518, the tribesmen brought highly polished copper axes with painted wooden handles, which the Spanish soldiers thought were made of gold of low grade quality. Accordingly, within three days the Europeans acquired some six hundred of these weapons, giving in exchange green and white glass beads which the Indians thought were jade, a stone which they valued very highly. The chronicler[1] of this little episode said "We were very well contented, thinking that they were of debased gold, and the Indians were even more contented with their beads, but it was no good to either party, for the axes were made of copper, and the beads were valueless."

But, as I noted in a previous paragraph, it didn't take the Indians long to evaluate the quality of the trade goods offered in exchange for furs. Among the items given to the Delaware Indians of Pennsylvania by William Penn, Aug. 2, 1685, were: guns, tomahawks, glass bottles, kettles, pewter spoons, tobacco tongs, tobacco pipes, steels, flints, scissors, looking glasses, combs, jews harps, small wooden boxes, beads, wampum, knives, needles, red lead, blankets, strouding, awl blades, salt, sugar, tobacco, etc.

During the 17th century great quantities of cotton cloths were exported from the various provinces of India and which found their way, via the different European traders into North America.[2] These were sold by the piece, which around 1669-1679 was a bolt of cloth from 38 to 40 yards in length. Printed calicoes were termed "painted cloths" or "paintings". Calico was the generic term for all cotton cloths in the 17th century. Rumals, Romals or Rammals were kerchiefs, as were Sannis, Cassas, Demeties (dimity). Chint was painted calico and the plural was chintz. Many of the terms were derived from the town or factory which produced it. The "factory" was a trading post, which term is still used by the Hudson's Bay Company.

Trade goods shipped from London to the Hudson's Bay Company posts in the 1670s included: tinsel lace, red Glocester cloth, red and blue Kersey cloth, coats and caps, powder horns, burning glasses, twine, gun powder, yarn stockings, brass rings, beads, scimitars, rings of brass wire, thread, kettles, calico shirts, knives.[3]

In the 18th century many more items were being supplied by the traders, particularly in the southern Appalachian country and inland around the Great Lakes and down the Mississippi Valley, where French, British and Spanish were playing power politics, using the Indians as pawns.

Among the French in Louisiana in 1714 the following objects were received from the mother country for trade with the tribes of the lower Mississippi Valley: pocket knives with horn handles made by Flatin, a cutler at Saint Etienne; small guns ornamented with brass, large white olive shaped beads, awls, light swords with ivory hilts, iron wire large as sail twine, and brass wire of the same dimension in ten pound coils, large shears, axes, pickaxes, fire steels, blue olive shaped beads, "Siamese style" pocket knives with wood handles, baize cloth of English manufacture, different colored French cloth from Rouen, Brittany linens, cloth of gold, boxwood combs, finest vermilion, etc.[4]

The British authorities in the Georgia Colony during the 1740s and 1750s distributed the following to their red children: Barrels of FF gunpowder, bullets and swan drop shot, Indian guns, paints, vermilion, rose, green, yellow; duffel cloth, gun flints, beads of all sizes, "stone ear rings", brass kettles (wired and bailed); spring knives; razors, looking glasses and scissors; tin pots, tin kettles (by the nest); hats, brass wire; coats and waistcoats; shirts of different patterns (check, garlisx, etc.); saddles, serge, calico and tobacco.[5]

In the 1770s the traders at Ft. Michilimackinac, Michigan, had in stock such things as beaver hats, green tea, molasses, spectacles, red hackle feathers, playing cards, fiddle strings, ruffled shirts and shoe buckles. Then too there were hawk bells, brass rings, clasp knives, butcher knives, trunks, candles, flints, brass jews harps, soap, coffee, scalping knives, beads, pewter basins, oil cloths, bridles, decanters, China ware, rum, wine and tobacco, in addition to all sorts of ribbons, textiles and other odds and ends.[6]

I cite these various lists of goods to indicate the trend of preferences on the part of the Indians in the different areas. In the far north around the Hudson's Bay special attention was given to ice chisels, iron harpoon heads, axes and knives, as well as good flint lock guns. From the 17th century onward there was a constant insistence on the part of the factors at the HBC posts for a better grade of well-tempered steel axes, knives, chisels, etc. The extremely cold temperatures played havoc with the metal tools and weapons and the smiths of Sheffield, while past masters of the art of tempering, seemed unable to understand the need for tempered edges that would withstand the sub-zero weather.

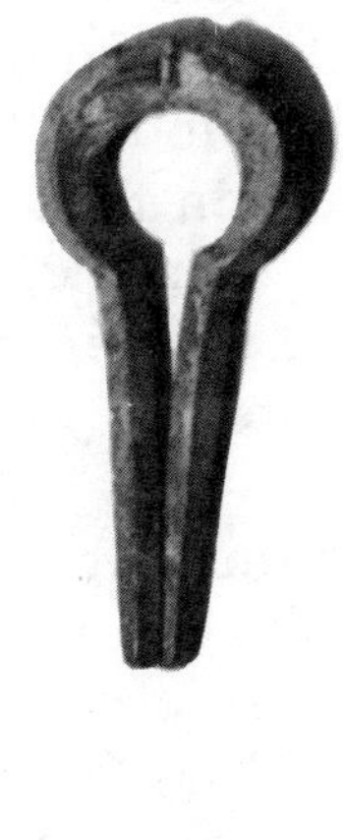

JEWS-HARP

As the trade expanded farther and farther, to the west and north, new tribes were encountered whose methods of living differed from those of the east and south. On the Plains, the Indians were not trappers, nor did the Indians of the Rocky Mountains use the steel trap to any great extent. These tribesmen were hunters and killed the buffalo, deer, elk, antelope, bear, and other such animals with bow, lance, and gun. The trappers of this region were the

Europeans. As a result trading methods varied somewhat. There were more brass and cheap junk jewelry. The use of good silver bracelets, rings, crosses, ear wheels, ear bobs, nose rings, arm bands, etc., was limited, except for the Upper Missouri where they were more common.

PEACE MEDAL

Silver medals, however, were still a part of the official intercourse between the governments of Great Britian, United States, Spain, and Russian, and the various tribes of Indians falling under the jurisdiction of those respective governments.

To go into the ramifications of the trade in each area would necessitate a volume or volumes, hence in this chapter on trade goods I propose to detail only such items as seem pertinent to the area in the Northwest.

GLASS BEADS

The common denominator of the trade beginning in the 16th century was the lowly glass bead. A few facts concerning these beads are given in the following paragraphs.

In general, the bulk of the glass beads traded on the North American continent from the 16th until around the first half of the 19th centuries were made in the glass factories of Murano, Venice. Oddly enough in the many references to glass manufacture, there is no single volume dealing with glass beads alone. The references to the methods of making these colorful baubles are widely scattered, mostly in isolated articles in various periodicals.

Nomenclature of glass beads is likewise as varied as the beads themselves and is derived from a number of different sources. The Italian manufacturers had special names for certain kinds of beads. The distributors, wholesale and retail, likewise applied different terms to different sizes and colors of beads. The traders in ordering beads had their own system of nomenclature and finally the collector of beads in our own times has added to the confusion by calling beads by local terms, which outside that area have little or no meaning.

There is one common error in the classification of glass beads made by traders, authors and collectors alike which needs clarification at this time. That is the use of the word "porcelain" as applied to the opaque glass beads. Charles Yriarte[7] refers to such beads as "colored enamels" and refers to Dr. Salvati as his authority for the use of this term:

"Colored enamels are made of a vitreous paste or composition.

They are composed of the same substance, silicious or otherwise, as ordinary glass; but to these are added other mineral ingredients, which, properly prepared and mixed, give the paste its density, extreme hardness and color. It is by these means that the desired opacity, the purity and solidity of the enamels, their beauty, the softness and great variety of their color are obtained. These different qualities depend as much on the quantity and quality of the mineral elements which are combined with those of ordinary glass as on the degree of continuous heat to which the composition is subjected during its fusion." Thus, all of those beads which are opaque white, red, yellow, blue, green or black and which in general are called "porcelain beads", are in effect "colored enamels".

But to pursue further the use of the word "porcelain" in connection with beads listed on 17th-19th century trade lists, there were "porcelain" beads in Europe long before the ceramic ware by that name was introduced from the Orient. The term however is derived from the Latin-Italian porcellana after porcella, "little pig", which name was applied to the Venus shell (according to one authority) and to the Mediterranean cowrie, according to another, because these shells by reason of their rounded appearance resembled a pig's back.

According to Edna Kenton,[8] "Porcelain (a word of Italian origin: adopted with slight variations into nearly all European languages) was a name given from very early times to a univalvular, gastropodus mollusk, Cypraea; especially used for the species C. moneta, the money cowry of Africa and the East Indies and for its shell. The same term was applied to the nacre (from which were made vases, ornaments, etc.) obtained from the shells of this and many other mollusks; and the enameled pottery brought from the Orient about the 16th century was also called 'porcelain', from its resemblance to this nacre."

Strings of "porcelain beads" were sold in the apothecary shops in France for medicinal purposes. The beads were pulverized in mortars for their lime content and administered in wine, water, etc. In turn the French explorers and traders among the Iroquois, Algonquin, etc. referred to the strands, strings, belts, collars, etc., of shell wampum beads used by those Indians of the 17th century as "porcelain beads". Scholars translating the French publications inferred that these shell beads were the ceramic porcelain beads, and so the word porcelain came to be applied to the opaque glass beads so common to the trade during the late 18th and early 19th centuries. Thus, in general, when collectors and students refer to the opaque glass beads as "porcelain" they are in error. The bulk of all beads, aside from the metallic beads, shell beads, stone or wood beads, traded to the Indians were made of glass.

Perhaps a brief description of the manufacture of glass beads might be appropriate.

Yriarte states:[9] "Murano was the centre of this beautiful art of glass manufacture...the Muranese industry went back at least as far as the eleventh century...In the thirteenth century the art takes a further development; in 1268 the glass workers are already formed into a corporation...The furnaces at that time were on the Rialto; a police measure decreed by the Grand Council orders that they shall be destroyed for fear of fire, and reconstructed in the neighborhood of Venice (8th November, 1291). Some glass workers had already established themselves at Murano and those who were not ejected from Venice joined them, and the glass manufacture soon became the specialty of the island."

To discourage the art of glass working from spreading to other countries by the disaffection of the glass makers, the Senate of the Republic of Venice in 1673, through the Inquisitors, issued this decree: "If any workman or artist transports his art into a foreign country to the detriment of the Republic, he shall be sent an order to return; if he does not obey, his nearest relatives shall be imprisoned, so as to reduce him to obedience by his interest in them; if he returns the past will be pardoned and an establishment in Venice will be procured for him; and if, in spite of the imprisonment of his relatives, he is still determined to live abroad, an emissary will be charged to kill him, and after his death his relatives will be set at liberty."

This 26th article of the statutes of the State Inquisitors was the result of the defection of a group of workmen who had been induced by the French ambassador in Venice to flee into France to begin glass making in that country.[10]

The same author states: "Glass beads, which are so varied in their character, and which were at first simply round and blue, white, green or red colored, but later were covered with enamels, gold, bronze or opal color, have played an almost incredible part in commerce...Sought after everywhere, in Asia and on the borders of the Black Sea, these beads found their way even to the remote regions of central Africa, where in later times travelers have found them being used as money. The quantities that were scattered over the world are incalculable, and this simple bead of glass was a source of immense wealth to the Republic. She knew its value well, and if she were proud of her goblets and vases it was of her bead manufactories and bead trade that she was the most jealous...The corporations of glass workers already formed divided themselves into special classes: the verixelli, who made the small glass objects such as beads, the phioleri, who made bottles...Beads, which played an important part in business became a source of wealth to Venice, and an element of commerce with the distant countries, became richer and more varied; they constitute a special branch of the industry carried on by a separate corporation, the 'Paternostri a rosette' and 'Oldani' -- names which are still in use."[11]

In April, 1856, a correspondent for the Scientific American, who signed himself simply "JPB", wrote an article "Venetian Glass--How They Make Beads", which appeared in the issue of June 14, 1856, in which he described the processes:

"The great renown that Venice has obtained for glass works is chiefly owing to the immense number of beads manufactured in its establishments. Having visited all the large factories here, I will endeavor to describe the process.

"The materials are put into smaller furnaces than those used in America but constructed upon the same principle, with the contrivances for economizing fuel for which the Italians are celebrated.

"When the mass is sufficiently fused the coloring pigment is thrown in and mixed with the molten glass. When thoroughly amalgamated the workman gathers a couple of pounds of the metaled matter upon the end of an iron rod which he withdraws from the furnace and manipulates upon an iron slab; after this he plunges the glass into a tub of water. When it is sufficiently cooled he sticks it into the furnace again where it remains until melted; then it is taken out and fashioned into a shape resembling a bottle, with the bottom broken out.

"Another workman now brings a similar lump attached to another rod; the two are welded together; then a couple of boys take each one of the rods and 'travel' in opposite direction to either end of a long shed. As these boys run away from each other, the glass is drawn out into long tubular wires, so to call them, and lies along ground, where it is suffered to remain until cooled, after which it is broken up in lengths or tubes three feet long and sold to bead and bugle makers (a distinct class of operatives) or sent into other rooms of the same establishment where workmen break them into minute particles.

"This operation is performed by men, women and boys--who have before them an iron gauge into which with one hand they thrust fifteen or twenty tubes at the same time, and with an iron instrument (resembling a hatchet head) in the other hand, they rapidly chop off the ends of the tubes, according to the size adjusted to the gauge. The cuttings are then taken below where they are put into an iron barrel along with some sand and placed in a furnace over a pretty hot fire. A boy gives a revolutionary motion to the barrel until the sharp edges are properly shaped, when they are taken out of the barrel and polished by being poured into bags and shaken from side to side by the force of two men--in the same manner I have seen people in this country cleaning coffee and grain.

"After polishing, the beads are sifted into sizes and then some men with light wooden trays sort out the perfect specimens by a peculiar jerking motion and slant which they dexterously give to the tray. The refuse is melted over again and now the finished beads are put upon strings by a number of girls employed for that purpose.

"Various sizes are produced by larger or smaller tubes as the case may be, but in all the operation is the same, the sifting process being necessary on account of the unevenness of the original tubes. The colors were very brilliant in some instances, but in all cases the glass seemed full of grits and blemishes until toned down by the action of the fire in the second furnace.

"Many large warehouses receive the beads, where they are packed away in boxes for exportation. In one warehouse I saw several hundred tuns (sic) of them, filling barrels and boxes, or strings of them piled away on shelves in compartments occupied by various colors. They were of all sizes from the minutest mustard seed to the immense egg-like articles, exported to Africa and the Indies, for the use of the dusky beauties of those climes."

TRADE BEADS

In spite of his close observations the author did not mention the fact that when the cut beads were placed in the annealing barrel a mixture of sand and wood ashes was used also. Another article on bead making[12] states:

"In making beads small tubes of vari-colored glass were drawn out very long and thin. Then these were cut into smaller cylinders and these were placed in a mixture of sand and wood ashes and stirred until the tiny cylinders assumed smooth rounded forms. The beads were then removed and the holes cleaned out. A more modern method (1882) was in a bead making furnace. Sections of the small tubes were placed in a hot iron drum which was rotated over a fire just hot enough to keep the glass plastic without melting it. In this fashion the beads were rounded."

So much for the technical processes in the manufacture of the ordinary glass beads. As noted, some beads were cut and polished by hand. These crystal beads were more expensive than others. There were other faceted beads made by the simple method of holding the small segments of glass tubes against an abrasive wheel for a split second and the facets were made in this fashion. These have an uneven appearance but are not as uneven as the hand molded faceted beads which appear during the 17th century which have the appearance of having been roughly faceted by a small metal spatula while the glass was in a semi-plastic shape.

All sources point toward Murano as the main manufacturing center for glass trade beads until the first half of the 19th century, at which time some beads were manufactured in France and some in Czechoslovakia, known then as Bohemia. Other countries imported beads from Italy and repackaged them for shipment abroad. This was done in England, Belgium, France, etc. Likewise certain type beads which were widely circulated by the different fur companies were known by the names of those outfits, thus the red and white beads which were traded in great quantities by the Hudson's Bay Company in western Canada and on the Northwest coast, as well as in the upper reaches of the Yukon, were called "Hudson's Bay beads". Other beads, such as the large ultra marine blue faceted beads found along the coast of southern Alaska and British Columbia and as far south as Washington and Oregon, became "Russian beads", in spite of the fact that original packages of these beads, wrapped in grey coarse paper, were found unopened in the warehouse of the Russian American Fur Company at Sitka in 1867, marked "Brussels". In the latter case it was probably a repackaging job done by an export company in the Belgian city.

Beads were sent into the field packaged in different ways. Some beads sold bulk, by the pound, and were sent in casks, barrels or boxes. Others were strung, particularly the smaller varieties. The latter were sold by the mass, or by the French traders in the 18th century by the _brasse_. This was a French linear measurement of 5.318 feet but in the trade of the 18th century it was used to indicate a shorter measure, perhaps the length of a forearm, around 18 inches. The French _Noveau Larousse_ dictionary states that the term originally indicated a measure obtained by extending the arms and taking the distance between the two outstretched hands. A small _brasse_ was five feet, a large _brasse_ was six feet. Strands of both glass and shell (porcelain) or wampum beads were thus measured. A mass of beads contained about a dozen strands.

The nomenclature of the various kinds of beads originated at the glasshouses. There was, for example, a type of bead known as the "star" or "chevron bead" made of polychrome glass arranged in layers. The exterior layer was either blue or green and the ends formed a star pattern of about 12 points. These were known to the makers as "paternosters" or "Our Fathers" and the men who made them were also called by that name. These beads range in a variety of sizes from the large ones two inches and upward in length and 1-1/2 inches in diameter to quite small ones. At times these beads are almost round. The medium and large sized ones usually taper toward each end, giving the appearance of having been roughly whittled like a school boys pencil. The chevrons or star patterns are usually in red and white with a dark blue exterior lined with longitudinal white pin stripes. Such beads are generally found on 16th and 17th century sites, although I believe there was a revival of this style in Venice in the early 20th century. As a matter of fact, a number of the earlier 17th-18th and early 19th century type beads were made in the 1890's and even well into the 20th century, but these have only a pseudo-resemblance to the originals.

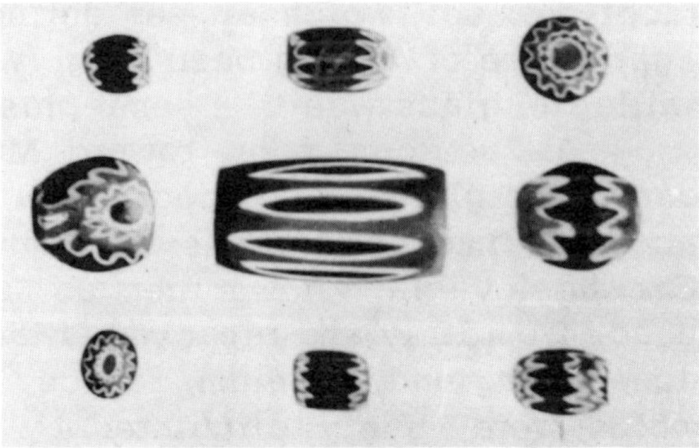

PATERNOSTER BEAD

In the middle to late 1850s many of the beads which found their way into the hands of the Indians were also being used by white women to bead many articles.

The popular faceted beads which are found on old village sites and in Indian burials of the 1830s-1860s, and even into the 1870s, in clear translucent colors, crystal, amber, blue and green, were known to the trade as "O.P." beads.

Thousands of these beads have been found in burials all the way from Alaska and western Canada, through the upper plains country and the full length of the San Joaquin Valley in California, the heaviest concentration of them being in the upper part of the San Joaquin and the adjacent foothills.

Although the white women used them in making mats and table covers and as pendant strands on chandeliers and flower vases, the Indian women worked them into necklaces, or sewed them individually on dresses and made fringes of them for their cloth and skin garments. They were sold in bunches or masses of twelve strands each. They were also called short "bugles".

Bugle beads, so named in the early days of the trade, assumed quite different proportions at different times. During the 17th century these bugles ranged in length from half an inch to delicate thin walled tubes of opaque glass more than three inches in length and as small as 1/16 inch in diameter. These early bugle beads are seldom found on other than 17th century sites in parts of New York, New Jersey, Pennsylvania and southeastern Canada. In color they range from opaque white, opaque dull, reddish brown, opaque light and dark blue and black. Occasionally they are roughly rectangular in cross section, or they may have a spiral twist to them. Sometimes the solid color is relieved with longitudinal pin stripes of opaque white, black or red lines. Again they may be of a dull red exterior with a dark green, almost black looking, translucent interior lining, or an opaque light blue bead may have a translucent blue lining.

In later periods, late 18th and early 19th centuries, the bugle beads assumed different aspects. In general they were much shorter and never reached the length of the 17th century bugles, and in color they ranged from crystal clear through clear light and dark blue, green, amber, and sometimes tinted inside with yellow, pink, blue, etc. The dull red color of the 17th century continued on into the 19th century, as did the translucent dark green lining. In the 1850s, short white "satin" bugles were used along with jet black thin bugles of very small diameters.

During the 18th century, particularly in the Hudson's Bay region, the bugles were called "rods". Around 1853-1854, a type of bugle beads, green, purple, bronze or blue was introduced from Bohemia. These were sold by the ounce or pound. The price 6 pence per ounce was considered a "fair price". These varied in length and diameter, but many of the ones used in trimming garments were short and fine. Among the white women these little bugles, black and white, were used on mourning clothes. Women purchasers of bugles in the 19th century were advised to select only those beads that were bright and smooth and not too fine in the pipe. The common lengths of these mid-19th century bugles were from one-eighth to one-third of an inch. In 1854, popular colors were black, white, gray, green, purple and pink.

The usual run of small beads used in ornamenting cloth or skin garments were termed "seed beads". The smallest of these were exceedingly tiny and although they found some favor in the 17th century, the use of these beads was not revived on any great scale until the opening of the 19th century. Because of the minute apertures, special jeweler's needles were needed to string these beads on very fine thread. The Indian had one advantage in this respect. Sinew thread can be made very fine and is tough and the end of the thread can be made to serve as a needle to pick up the beads, but a regular needle or fine awl was used to pierce the cloth or leather. These beads were sold in small hanks of about ten strands each.

Other small beads, of the larger variety of seed beads, were known as "pound beads" because they were sold in that manner. Certain sizes of these were known to the trade and to collectors today as "pony beads" or "pony trader" beads. The latter names were allegedly given because the first traders penetrating the western wilds carried their stocks of trade goods on pack ponies. In my estimation, however, this term is a misnomer for the reason that these coarse opaque beads, white, black, red, blue, etc., were not the only style beads being traded to the Indians at that period, which was in the opening decades of the 19th century. As a matter of fact, these same beads had been long a trade product.

"Cut beads" supplied to the Indians were those beads cut or faceted on angles and reflected the light better than the other beads. Such beads were usually found in ruby, black, garnet, crystal, green and blue or amber colors. In effect these "cut beads" were similar to the "short bugles", with this exception: the segments of glass tubing from which the beads were originally made were shorter and the facets more numerous and cut at sharper angles.

In fact, in some instances about the only distinction that can be made between certain types of "short bugles" and "cut beads" is the expense of original tubing as it appears unmarred by the cutter's tool. Careful examination of the bugles will show that only the ends of the tube segments have been faceted. Thus, one might say that both the "short bugles" and the multi-faceted beads are "cut beads". Many of the latter assume a semi-round shape completely covered with minute facets. These beads may range from a quarter of an inch or even less to three quarters of an inch in diameter. Many of the latter size, a dark, rich ultra-marine blue, are found on Russian sites in Alaska in conjunction with the large tubular faceted beads one-half inch in length and half an inch in diameter. The latter are of the same color but have only about six or seven small facets cut on each end in contrast to the eleven sloping facets cut on each end and a triple row of smaller facets cut around the center of the bead, making a total of 55 facets cut on one bead.

FACETED BEADS

A pseudo-effect of the multiple facets is noted on the light opaque blue beads. Here we see seven facets cut on each end, leaving the center row of facets formed by the uncut surface of the bead. The shortness of the original segment of tube is responsible for the ultimate effect.

"Fancy Beads". Under this terminology fall many beads, infinite in variety and form. The term has been used since the early part of the 19th century, and possibly earlier, although in the 1770s certain of these beads were called "flowered beads". In general the "fancy beads" were those which were inlaid with various motifs in colored glass against a solid background of white, black, blue, red, etc., or were overlaid with thin threads of raised glass in an aimless pattern. Certain of these would be covered with a number of round dots of glass inlaid like a mosaic; others had the clear glass dots raised in relief against a gilt or clear glass base.

POLYCHROME BEADS

Other beads in this category were composed of glass threads, satiny in effect or clear or opaque, spiraled around the perforation. Collectors call these "wire laid".

During the first three decades of the 19th century and on into the 1860s, many varieties of the "inlaid" fancy beads were traded from the Plains country, north and west to the Pacific Coast. Of all the tribesmen on the Plains, I believe the Crow were the ones who preferred these beads above all others. They used them on necklaces and as adornment offerings attached to their buffalo medicine bundles.

In England in the 18th century these "flowered" beads were called by various names. There was one bead with a grey-white background inlaid with round eyelets or dots of white against the grey background and the centers of these eyelets were either red or blue. These beads were called "Kitty Fisher's Eyes", after a noted English actress who died in 1767. Other beads of a similar type were called "Pompadour" after the noted mistress of Louis XV of France. Still others, because of a multitude of colors, were termed "Paisleys" after the shawls of that name. Although the bulk of these beads were made in Murano, there was a time in the early 1800s when raw glass tubes ready for cutting into "fancy" beads, were shipped into Bristol, England, where they were converted into beads. Such beads in England were used as weights on lace bobbins and were called jingles, gingles or spangles.[13] They were in use in the English midlands, Northamptonshire, Bedfordshire and Buckinghamshire, nine to a bobbin being the credited number. Other types of "fancy beads" were those which were round and plain glass, silvered or gilt to look like gold and silver beads. The small, flat circular gold and silver sequins were also included under the term "fancy beads".

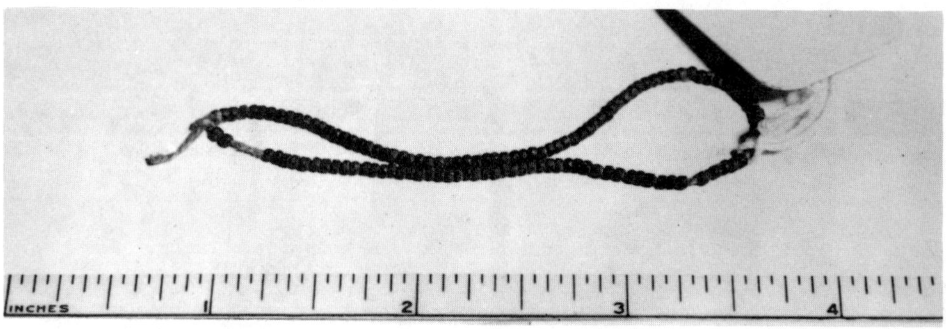

FACETED METAL BEADS

During the 19th century, tiny faceted as well as round, plain, metal beads, gilt, silvered and shining polished and blued steel beads were used. Occasionally one finds these beads on Indian sites, although they were not too popular among the natives. The round brass beads of varying sizes, as well as copper beads, were more favored by the tribesmen.

However, in other portions of the Lewis and Clark Journals more data are given on these beads. One entry says: "Blue beads. This is a coarse cheap bead imported from China and costing in England 15^{d} the lbs. in strands. It is far more valued than the white beads of the same manufacture and answers all the purposes of money, being counted by the fathom.[14]

Judging by the types of blue and white beads which have been found in the Columbia river basin, these blue beads of the "coarse variety" mentioned by the American pioneer explorers, are the opaque, light sky blue beads, round and smooth of varying sizes and the smooth, round, chalk white opaque beads of corresponding sizes.

Although they are called "China beads" and were noted as such on the trade lists, I am not at all convinced that they originated in the country of China. I believe this term was applied to these beads because of the fancied resemblance to the "China ware", i.e., smooth ceramic wares made in various countries which took on the name "China" because that country had supplied the first porcelain wares a hundred or more years earlier.

Trade began on the Northwest Coast in the last quarter of the 18th century. Stray vessels may have reached the area during the 16th and 17th centuries but no active trading was carried on. There is always the possibility however of objects from those earlier times being recovered from Indian sites in the region, but in the main, the material which has been recovered by archeologists and collectors in the 20th century may be said to date from the 1770s onward. Extensive and heavy trading was carried on by ships of different nationalities in the late 1780s and early 1790s. The Spanish, French, English, American and Russian traders all vied with one another in the race to drain the coastal tribes of the rich harvest of sea otter, seal, and other furs. Some of these European ship masters loaded up with goods in Europe or bought them from firms in China and elsewhere in the Orient. Hence one may expect to find in the cultural debris left in the wake of these long ago traders, anything from Chinese coins to Venetian beads and Spanish weapons.

CHINESE COINS

So rich was the field that not only did the more substantial items such as axes, buttons, beads, kettles, guns, swords, knives, etc., find their way into native hands in exchange for furs, but other things like rice, molasses, flour and even other furs, elk skins and abalone shells and the European and Oriental species of the dentalia became articles of trade.

A volume might be written on the various kinds of goods and the conflict between the various traders.

But to revert for a moment to the bead situation. I have already mentioned the deep, rich ultra-marine beads traded in the area. These beads, at least some of them, in spite of their size, are astonishingly fragile so it is no wonder that the Indians sometimes complained of this fragility.

In summing up the trade relations of the Indians residing along the Columbia River, Meriwether Lewis described the different tribes, the food they ate, and the skins of otter, elk, beaver, fox, etc., which they traded for objects of European manufacture:

"In return they receive guns (which are principally old British or American muskets) powder, ball and shot, copper and brass kettles, brass teakettles and coffee pots, blankets, from two to three points, coarse scarlet and blue cloth, plates and strips of sheet copper and brass, large brass wire, knives, tobacco, fish-hooks, buttons and a considerable quantity of sailors hats, trousers, coats and shirts. But, as we have had occasion to remark more than once, the object of foreign trade which is most desired are the common cheap, blue or white beads, of about fifty or seventy to the pennyweight, which are strung on strands a fathom in length, and sold by the length of both arms: of these blue beads, which are called tia commashuck, or chief beads, hold the first rank in their ideas of relative value. The most inferior kind are esteemed beyond the finest wampum, and are temptations which can always seduce them to part with their most valuable effects.[15] Indeed, if the example of civilized life did not completely vindicate their choice, we might wonder at their infatuated attachment to a bauble in itself so worthless. Yet these beads are, perhaps, quite as reasonable ob-

ROLLED BEADS MADE BY THE INDIANS FROM TRADE SHEET COPPER

jects of research as the precious metals, since they are at once beautiful ornaments for the person and the great circulating medium of trade with all the nations on the Columbia."

In this single paragraph Lewis epitomizes the trade on the Columbia, indicating the type of goods carried to the Indians of that region and establishing the blue and white beads as the common denominators of that trade.

The term used to set these beads apart from the other beads carried by the party is rendered tia commashuck in this instance and again (Id. p. 272) "tiacomoshack or chief beads". This term is composed of two words in the Chinook jargon, tyee, tai, tie, tye tyeyea or tyhee, as it was spelled phonetically by those who heard it, and the word kamosuk or bead. The first word does mean "chief" but in this case it probably also means "superior", hence was not intended to denote beads meant for a Chief alone but to mean "the beads superior to all others", "the tyee or chief among the beads".[16]

TRADE ON THE NORTHWEST COAST

As previously noted, trade goods varied according to the whims of the natives. An item that might be in demand one year might be rejected in the following year. The colors and sizes of beads were usually dictated by the aboriginal color schemes prevalent in these regions as well as the modes of decorating either the person or garments in aboriginal times.

Thus, a group of people who had been in the habit of using porcupine quill work on dresses, shirts, leggings, moccasins, gun scabbards, etc. might be expected to accept the finer seed beads as a substitute for the quills. Those Indians who did not need these small beads for such purposes might accept eagerly the larger beads for necklaces or even for adornment of other objects.

IRON CHISEL

Color symbolism was strong among many tribes. Usually, these colors were associated with religious beliefs. Many tribes did not differentiate too strongly between blue and green. Each direction of the compass was denoted by a different color, hence the basic colors of white, blue, red, green, black and yellow were accepted without question. At times it is difficult to obtain satisfactory answers to the questions why certain colors are preferred above all others without extensive ethnological research. In other cases the problem is solved more easily. Colors associated with emotions, such as white for peace, red for war, black for death, are relatively simple, hence the use of the fine white seed beads among the Iroquois where white was a peaceful color. On the other hand white beads among the tribes along the Columbia river and elsewhere in the northwest, extending along the coast of Alaska and even into the Eskimo country, went begging. In those areas blue was the color most in demand, ranging through all shades of light, medium and dark. Lewis and Clark in their wanderings along the Columbia soon discovered that a blue bead of any size would be eagerly accepted, while red could scarcely be given away. White was also a favorite color.

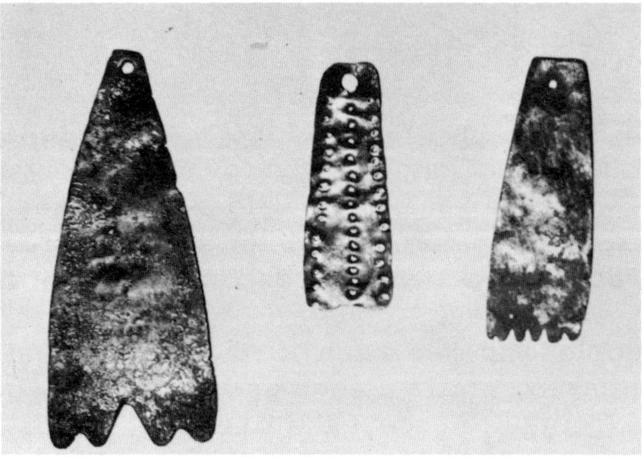

INDIAN MADE COPPER BANGLES

BRASS DRAWER PULL USED FOR A BANGLE

In such instances then it would seem that the preferences were not mere whimsical vagaries but were based upon some fundamental beliefs of the people themselves. Time after time the American explorers on their first trip across the continent, 1804-1806, noted the preferences for blue beads voiced by the Columbia river tribesmen.

John McLoughlin, writing to his superiors of the HBC from his post at Ft. Vancouver, July 6, 1827, detailing various Company affairs mentioned the quality of goods received that year and said:

"The Aqua Marina Coliers do not suit the fancy of the natives; they complain of their being brittle, the Beads sent as a sample to England (and as a substitute for which these Coliers have been sent) was imported from China and cost only twenty eight Dollars p. picul" (Chinese weight, 133 1/3 lbs.).[17]

Another note on beads ordered from China is found in Vol. X, id. Simpson's "Journey to the Columbia", 1828, p. 143. In this instance the Hudson's Bay Company officials in London wrote to Messrs. Perkins & Co., Canton, China:

"I am also to request you will be pleased to procure and forward in such manner as you may consider most advisable 'Five hundred weight' Beads of the inclosed sample as they are such as you were formerly in the habit of purchasing for Messrs. McTavish & Compy."

By these two extracts it would appear that some beads were being shipped from China by European companies. As yet however I have not encountered any statement which says these beads were manufactured in China. The British maintained large mercantile firms in the Orient at this time and through their godowns flowed merchandise from all quarters of the globe, hence there is the possibility that these beads "from China" had been shipped in from Italy and were being redistributed. China as a country was not a great glass manufacturing or exporting nation. I have seen beads which are said to have been made in China during the 20th century but these have a different appearance than those from European glass houses.

Another variety of bead which was widespread in the latter part of the first half of the 19th century is the "Cornaline d'Aleppo", so named because it was associated in the Italian export business with the city of Aleppo in the Near East.

The major characteristics of these beads are distinct differences between the exterior and interior finishes. In one style the exterior is a bright translucent or semi-translucent red, while the core is either opaque white, pale yellow or pink. The bulk of the interiors is white with yellow a close second. These beads are found in a variety of sizes, large ovoid, flattened circular or tubular, and round, in varying sizes. Another bead in this category is cylindrical but it appears to have found favor mainly among the tribes of the upper San Joaquin Valley in California, particularly among those peoples who traded with the coastal Pomo. These cylindrical beads are on the average 5/8ths of an inch long and approximately 5/16ths of an inch in diameter. Thus, in appearance, size and color, so far as the exterior finish is concerned, they approximate the aboriginal bead manufactured of magnesite by the Pomos and traded in prehistoric as well as early historic times to their neighbors in the valley and eastern slopes of the Sierra Madre. During the 1840s-1860s, the white men began obtaining supplies of these glass imitation magnesite beads in great quantities, and the making and distribution of the stone beads began tapering off much to the dismay of the Pomo manufacturers. The values dropped of course as the supplies of the glass beads increased in volume. Thus we find the distribution of these particular beads in a relatively limited area, although the other forms of the same bead were widespread from the Athapascan tribes of western and northwestern Canada, Alaska, and well down into the Northern Plains country, as well as Washington, Oregon, California and elsewhere in the west where beads were a regular media of exchange between whites and Indians.

Antedating the Cornaline d'Aleppo bead with the translucent red exterior and opaque white or yellow interior, and keeping chronological pace with its distribution into modern times, is the Cornaline d'Aleppo which has an opaque, dull reddish-brown exterior and a translucent dark green interior. In some cases the green is so dark as to appear on casual inspection as black. As yet, in all the thousands of examples I have not found a bead of this type with a black core, nor have I observed a Cornaline d'Aleppo with a translucent exterior and a translucent interior. These early type beads, opaque dull-reddish exterior, occur on sites of the 17th and 18th centuries in eastern Canada, ranging south into New York, Pennsylvania, and throughout the southern states. At times these 17th century beads will have inlaid opaque white, black, blue, etc. stripes in the exterior opaque coating and retain the dark green translucent core. In both types of the Cornaline d'Aleppo beads the sizes range from the long thin bugles to small seed beads.

Judging by comparative examples of both types of beads which I have seen from dated sites, north, east, south and west, I believe the ones with the opaque interiors and translucent exteriors fall more in the 19th century while the other style is found in greater proportions on the 17th and 18th century sites, although it lingered on into the 19th century in certain areas. To pinpoint the exact time of their appearance in the chronological scale, without further detailed research, is almost impossible at the present time.

As noted in previous paragraphs, the Indians, as do all other people, adopted new styles quickly in some instances and clung conservatively to others. Thus the Earl of Southesk, writing from Carlton House of the HBC on the Saskatchewan in July 1859, said "It amused me to see that fashion reigned here as imperiously as in more civilized lands; some fine, richly-coloured oval beads, the size of pigeon's eggs, which I considered my best, and which a year or two ago would have been generally admired, were despised and out of date, while the little trashy white ones, no bigger than a pin's head, were highly appreciated."

BRACELET DETAIL

A few years earlier the American Fur Company experienced the same shift in bead preferences in the period from 1833 when a shipment of "agate beads", ordered from the importing firm of Geisse & Korckhouse of Philadelphia, were not delivered on time and were not in fashion by January 1835. These beads were classed as "fancy beads" and although the importing firm tried to persuade the Company to accept these beads as late as 1836, the Company refused to buy them.[19]

By the same token, trade items other than beads, went in and out of favor very quickly. On the Northwest Coast in 1799, coastal Indians who traded with their neighbors on the interior, readily accepted muskets, blue and red broadcloth, powder, iron wire, axes, coarse cutlery and great coats. These Tlingit and Haida traders traveled as far as two and three hundred miles inland carrying the wares they had received from the white traders who came to the coast in ships. These native traders obtained skins from their red brethern and made profits of 200 to 300 per cent when they returned to meet the ships. There were times when price wars between rival white traders worked to the benefit of the Indian traders. At times, as in 1799, the ship traders ran short of muskets and one gun fetched 4 or 5 skins. At this same time 2 fathoms of red cloth equaled 3 fathoms of blue.

In this same year the master of the American ship ELIZA, Captain Rowan out of Boston, introduced the use of bread, rice and molasses to the Haida Indians at Kaigani village on Vancouver Island. These new foodstuffs took like wildfire and thereafter a bottle of molasses was accepted in lieu of one fathom of broadcloth when sea otter skins were bringing 3 fathoms of cloth, each. In 1800 the articles of trade were about the same, 3 fathoms of cloth equaled one sea otter pelt (the greatest price ever given on the coast); 2 fathoms usually were considered a fair trade for one skin. One hogshead of hard bread equaled 5 skins, or 8 gallons of rice and molasses for one skin. In 1800 also a thick type of strong woolen cloth known as "duffils" or "Duffels" (after the town of Duffel in the Low Lands where it was woven) was introduced into the trade on the coast and thereafter the Indians preferred that cloth to those which were thinner.

In 1801, $1,000 worth of rice and molasses equaled in value $10,000 worth of cloth so that by the end of that year the market was glutted with cloth as well as muskets, and in the following year no flintlocks could be traded unless they were the finest of fowling pieces or the best in regulation English arms. In fact the Indians at this time began trading guns back to the whites. The new foodstuffs, bread, rice and molasses, held firm.

The natives along the Columbia river in the late 18th century had quite a trade with the whites in "moose" or elk hides, which in turn were in great demand among the Tlingits and Haidas further north. Those people called these skins kas or klemmel and used them to make war jackets, which were practically impenetrable to anything but musket balls.[20]

It was Sturgis also who gave an interesting sidelight on the trade along the Northwest Coast for this same period. In 1802 he made a trip to that area and said that the price of large and small sea otter pelts laid down in Canton, China, at that time was $20. It was on this same trip that Sturgis discovered that the white ermine skins which were prized highly by the Haida, Tlingit, Kwakiutl, etc. for use on ceremonial masks, wands, garments, etc., were scarce and difficult to obtain. Accordingly he requested that the firm's agent in Europe be authorized to purchase as many of these weasel skins as possible at the annual fur fair held in Leipsic, Germany.

Some 5,000 such skins were bought for less than thirty cents each and in turn were traded in a single forenoon for 560 prime sea otter pelts in 1804, which then had a retail value of $50 apiece in Canton. He unloaded all of his ermine skins at the rate of five ermines for one otter. The next season and the following year (1806) the market was so glutted by rival traders that one hundred ermine would not bring one sea otter skin.

Abalone shells used as ornaments along the Northwest Coast, were likewise another item of trade brought in by the white men. The first of these California shells were carried to Nootka Sound in August 1774 by the crewmen on board the Spanish frigate <u>Santiago</u> alias <u>La Nueva Galicia</u>. These abalone had been gathered by the sailors from the rocks along the beach near Monterey and near the mouth of the Carmel river. One reason why the abalone from California were preferred is that the species of abalone which grows in the northern coastal waters is smaller, thin shelled, brittle and not as lustrous as the ones from further south.[22]

METAL PIPE

BELLS

Thus we see that the active trade between the white men and the Indians in the northwest, beginning in northern California and extending into Alaska, began around the last quarter of the 18th century and by the end of the 1700s was in full swing. The demand for sea otter skins continued unabated until well into the first half of the 19th century and during this period, of let us say approximately seventy-five years, hundreds of traders and thousands of all sorts of items of European manufacture poured into the area. It is only the barest residue of this volume of trade goods that has survived in burials, kitchen middens and old village sites to be salvaged by the archeologist and the amateur collector.

Naturally only those items of brass, pewter, silver, glass and ceramic wares have survived in the best condition. Now and then some object made of iron or steel is preserved in fair condition.

Even the glass mirrors seldom remain in good condition. The mercury on the reverse side peels off, leaving small circular disks or quadrilateral pieces of semi-iridescent glass. The iridescence on all glass is a sign of decay. Various chemical factors contribute toward the slow disintegration of glass beads, mirrors, bottles, etc.

Bronze, brass, silver and occasionally gold objects, such as buttons, portions of firearms, sword hilts, buckles, pins, kettles (both copper and brass), portions of the latter utensils, lock escutcheons, arm bands, wire bracelets, furniture fittings, and many other items too numerous to mention have been turned out by the spades of collectors and students.

The task of identifying many of these objects and placing them in correct chronological sequence is long and tedious. Unluckily like geometry, there is no "royal road" to the answers.

Among most tribes the choicest objects at the outset of their cultural contracts with the Europeans were made of metal. This is readily understandable. Any scrap of iron, steel, brass, bronze, copper, even tin, had its advantages over a tool made of stone, bone, shell, horn, antler, ivory or wood, for certain purposes.

Thus, to the Indian (who was non-hirsute) the few facial hairs were something to be removed. In his pre-European life he used clam shell pincers, hot embers, bits of obsidian, etc., to pluck or shave off the offending hairs. The introduction of steel, iron or brass wire springs made a much more convenient tool, hence we find short lengths of these springs in many Indian burials. The use of these springs in this manner would not occur to a white man because the operation was too painful, he had too many hairs, and it was simpler to use a razor and soap and water. In time the Indians used razors, but home-made pincers of wire springs or small bent pieces of tin, copper, brass, German silver, etc., served him equally as well.

THIMBLES PUNCHED TO MAKE TINKLERS

Thimbles, mostly of brass, are also found in great numbers. Here again Indian ingenuity was brought into play and the native women, by punching a small hole in the end and threading a thrum of buckskin through it with a single bead at one end, turned the thimble into a small bell or jingler with which she ornamented her dress, leggings, pouch, etc.

In turn, buttons of all types, flat, ball, convex, made of brass, silver, pewter, glass, pearl, bone, horn, German silver, cut steel, tin, iron, etc., were not used so much as garment fasteners as ornaments for parts of clothing, ceremonial regalia, blankets, robes, necklaces, etc. One encounters all types of buttons on old Indian sites.

The dating of metal buttons is difficult. One may only guess at the dates of certain buttons and be specific only in rare instances.

During the 18th century metallic buttons were made in two ways: they were cast in molds or stamped out by hand-operated (or foot) machines. In the course of button development, there was a period when most of these fasteners were made of cloth, silk thread or mohair over cardboard, wood or bone and horn bases. Around the middle of the 18th century in England, a type of button came into vogue which continued for the remainder of the 1700's and went into the 1800's. This was the "Shell button" which was composed of two parts. The face was a thin sheet or shell of silver, gold, brass (the latter being plain, silvered or gilt), which was in turn cemented to a base of wood, bone or cardboard. The design motifs on these buttons were indefinite, but during the 1750's through the 1780's it was fashionable to use "Shell buttons" bearing stamped imprints resembling the various patterns of the woven hair or silk buttons. Actually the metallic button industry in England took a spurt around 1670 and a button manufactory was established in Birmingham in 1689. Gilt buttons are said to have been made first by a man by the name of Taylor in Birmingham, England, in 1768. This early method of gilding was done by placing gold upon the base metal buttons, mixed with mercury, and the latter then driven off by heat, leaving a thin layer of gilt on the button, after which it was burnished.

By 1819, five grains of gold, worth one shilling, were sufficient to gild 144 buttons of one inch diameter. Metal buttons of brass, pewter, etc. were manufactured in the Colonies in North America as early as 1706, but the great button companies of New England (with few ex-

"COLONIAL" BUTTONS

ceptions) did not begin active operations until around 1800. Between the latter date and the mid-1830s, most of the large concerns such as Benedict & Burnham (which began as A. Benedict, 1823-1828, and as Benedict & Coe., 1829-1834), during which time they began to stamp their buttons "Treble Plate", "Extra Fine", "Double Gile", and "Superfine". This company of Aaron Benedict became the Waterbury Button Co. in 1849.

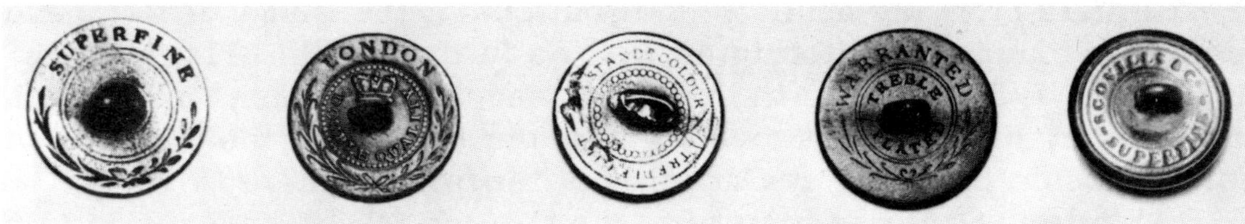

MARKS ON THE BACKS OF BUTTONS

This outfit manufactured many military buttons for the United States forces.

The Scovill Manufacturing Company, reputed to be "the oldest brass company in America", began business in 1802 as Abel Porter & Co. In 1811 it was Leavenworth, Hayden & Scovill, and in 1821 it was JML & WH Scovill. By 1840 it was Scovills & Co., and in 1850 it changed to Scovill Manufacturing Company. It is by studying the changes in the firm names in this manner that the dating of certain buttons becomes fairly certain.

In the matter of metallic military buttons, the first regimental numbers were placed on the buttons of the ordinary soldier's uniform by the French in 1762. This same system was adopted by the British in 1767. Even so, many officers during the 18th century used plain or stamped buttons (designs not necessarily military) on their uniforms, as did private soldiers. Hundreds of these buttons, plain, "shell" and stamped or engraved, have been found on military camp sites in the eastern part of the United States.

Later, when the uniforms changed and styles became obsolete, the latter garments were then passed on to the Indians, either as official gifts, or the private traders obtained them and sold them to good advantage.

In this manner many buttons of an earlier date have been found on Indian sites and in burials at a later period. Hence, care must be exercised in judging the date of a burial by the style or type of buttons found in it. The same admonition must hold true regarding trademarks on knives, axes, spear heads, guns, etc. In many cases the middle man in England, France, the United States or elsewhere bought unsigned articles and had his own firm name stamped thereon. One British concern which practiced this custom on a wide variety of articles was Jukes Coulson & Co. This was an export concern, not a manufacturing outfit.

One military button which has been found on Indian village sites and around California missions all the way from lower California to Oregon is that known as "the Phoenix button". These buttons, usually flat and circular, with various regimental numbers stamped on them below the figure of the Phoenix rising from the flames, have the inscription in French "Je Renais De Mes Cendres" (I Will Arise From My Ashes). Ball buttons of the same device have also been found in California as well as further north. Flat buttons, 5/8ths and 7/8ths inches in diameter, and ball buttons, 5/8th inch in diameter, have been recovered from the debris at the Mission of San Carlos de Borromeo at Carmel, not far from Monterey.

While the precise history of the buttons is not known, certain facts concerning them have been fitted together. It appears almost certain that these buttons were intended for the uniforms ordered by King Henri Christophe, the powerful Negro ruler of Haiti from 1811-1820. In the latter year however the Emperor committed suicide. It is believed that at the time of his death King Christophe had on order a quantity of new uniforms for his troops. The late Mr. Howland Wood, formerly the head of the American Numismatic Society in New York, was under the impression that the buttons, attached to uniform coats, had been ordered from New England merchants. When King Christophe died, all hope of collecting for the uniforms went by the board, and the coats were sold to traders engaged in the sea otter trade on the far Pacific Coast. Hence it is possible that these buttons could have found their way west during the 1820s and 1830s. They have turned up at Tumacacori Mission in southern Arizona, at San Juan Capistrano, San Luis Rey, Santa Barbara and Santa Ynez missions in southern California; at Carmel, as already noted, and at The Dalles in Oregon, as well as in the Yokuts cemetery at Elk Hill, Kern County, California, in the spring of 1935.[23]

The most popular type of brass button which was distributed far and wide among the plains, mountain and coastal Indians was the thin, flat brass button, in varying sizes from the large coat buttons to the small sleeve, and waist coat fasteners. When issued, these were usually gilt and presented a very flashy appearance, and as previously indicated, they were used almost entirely for ornaments by the Indians, unless attached to garments traded or sold to the tribesmen.

The earliest brass buttons were cast in one piece and the shank was a conical or wedge-shaped protuberance on the back. Later a wire loop was brazed on the back and until about 1860 the practice of buying the shanks from separate manufacturers and attaching them to the backs of the button blanks continued. Wire shanks were applied individually to these buttons with blow pipe and flux until around 1850. Likewise, since these early shanks made of wire were hand drawn, they were not perfectly round but tended to be oval in cross section.[24]

The history of button making is long and complex and it would be impossible in such a short article to trace the evolution of the button, as well as the myriad of types and the materials from which they were made. Occasionally one encounters references that are specific, but as a rule, the books written by button collectors are not the products of students. The collectors are more concerned with the accumulation of quantities of types, their condition, rarity, prices, etc., than in the historic technicalities that would enable one to make more precise definitions chronologically and otherwise.

Military buttons offer a better opportunity for dating than do those which were manufactured for general use, but even in that field many hours of tedious research are necessary to place the buttons themselves in their relations to the regulations.

These same observations hold true in regard to firearms, edged weapons and tools such as tomahawks, hand axes, broad axes, knives, daggers, etc. In fact, there is scarcely a single item from the lowly bead through the gun flints, clay pipes, fire steels, brass

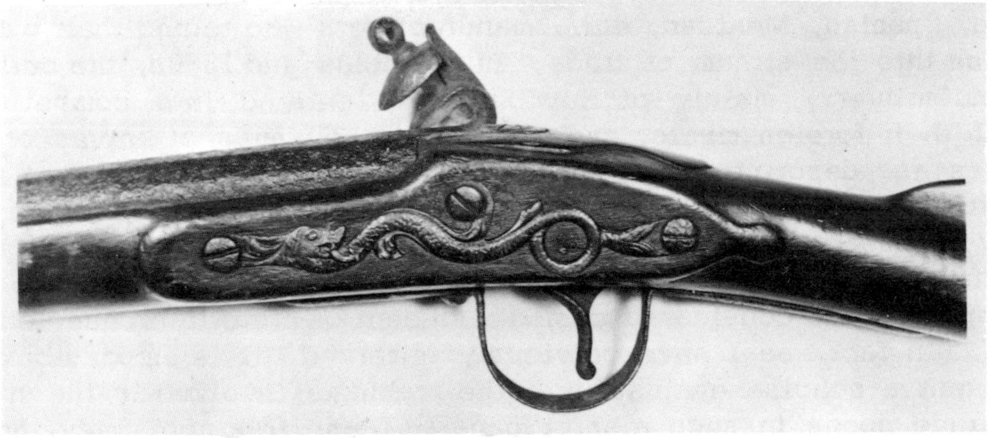

NORTH WEST TRADE GUN

and copper kettles, looking glasses, "hawks' bells", thimbles, pins, needles, etc., concerning which adequate histories have been written. The ordinary glass bottle is another subject which requires much study.

For example, there is one type of a patent medicine bottle which is found on the sites of the HBC posts in Canada, south into the trading posts and military forts of the Great Plains and in the Creek country in Alabama. This is the odd-shaped "Turlington's Balsam of Life" bottle. This particular bottle form, almost entirely covered with the letters of the raised inscription usually reading, "BY THE KINGS ROYAL PATENT GRANTED TO ROBT. TURLINGTON FOR HIS INVENTED BALSAM (or BALSOM) OF LIFE, JANUY 26, 1754, LONDON", was adopted by the maker of the Balsam in 1754, "to prevent the villainy of some persons, who, buying up my empty bottles, have basely and wickedly put therein a vile spurious counterfeit sort". This Balsam was advertised in brochures of 1755-57, and an American patent medicine under the same name continued in use for many years, and in the early 1900s, the Illinois Glass Company was manufacturing facsimiles of the 18th century Turlington bottle. American concerns sometimes copied these bottles exactly, and at other times slurred over the dates or omitted them entirely.[25]

In addition to Turlington's Balsam of Life, there were of course hundreds of other patent medicines, many of which originated in the United States in the first half of the 19th century and found their way into many strange places. Hence, to attempt anything like a comprehensive review of such containers at this time is impossible.

Cutlery traded to the Indians is another wide field. From the 17th century on to about the first three decades of the 19th century practically all of the knives made for the Indian trade came from abroad. During that period there were literally thousands of knife makers in Sheffield alone, not to mention the French, Belgian, German, Spanish, Mexican, etc., manufacturers who turned their wares loose into the stream of trade. In the 1820s and 1830s, the cutlery manufacturers, mainly of New England, entered into competition with their foreign rivals, and additional thousands of knives of all sizes and descriptions, with and without trade marks, were traded to the Indians, It would take years of study to classify and bring any semblance of order out of the chaos of cutlery manufacture and distribution. Similarly the brass and copper kettles offer another subject for the consideration of the student of historic archaeology.

In fact, as I have previously remarked, it is impossible to present a concise evaluation of the problems involved in the study of trade goods in such a short paper. These few notes may, however, provide the reader with some inkling of the enormous task ahead of those earnest students who are looking for new fields to conquer.

COPPER KETTLE

TOMAHAWK AND TRADE AXES

APPENDIX

Reprinted from

American Antiquity

Volume 25, No. 3, January 1960

PHOENIX BUTTONS

Emory Strong

Abstract

Metal buttons bearing the Phoenix bird, a motto in French, and a number are found in quantity in historic sites along the lower Columbia River, and less commonly throughout western North America. Phoenix buttons were not made for Napoleon, as often claimed, but were manufactured by an English firm in the early 1800's for King Christophe of Haiti. The Phoenix bird and the motto come from his coat of arms; the numbers refer to regiments. These military uniform buttons were brought to the Northwest before 1835 by an independent trader, most likely Nathaniel Wyeth, who probably used uniform coats, which he may have obtained earlier when shipping ice to the West Indies, to trade for fish for his salmon packing plant on the Columbia River.

ONE OF THE MOST interesting objects of historical archaeology is the Phoenix button, found in large numbers in the lower Columbia River valley and in much lesser quantities along the western coast and back into the plains. They have been excavated in mission sites in California and old village sites in the Southwest, one even in Mexico; they seem to have attained nearly nation wide distribution, although in small numbers. Specimens are in most of the large museums and are treasured in the show cases of many button collectors. But in spite of their extensive distribution their origin and history have never been completely traced.

The Phoenix button is found in three types, discs 0.95 and 0.60 inch in diameter, and a ball 0.65 inch in diameter. Each button bears a replica of the legendary Phoenix bird, the motto "Je Renais De Mes Cendres," and a number. The disc buttons are found in four different styles which I call styles 1, 2, 3, and 4 (Fig. 1). On each the motto is the same but the bird is different. The numbers, which are regiment numbers, run from 1 through 10, 14, 20, and 25 through 30 in the disc type, and 1 and 2 in the ball. Some numbers are quite rare; I know of only one number 3 large, numbers 10 and 14 large are quite rare but number 14 small is one of the most plentiful. Ball type buttons are very rare; I have seen only four but know that others have been found. The disc type is made of both brass and bronze, the ball type is copper and was once silver plated.

Style 1 (Fig. 1 *a*) large is found in all the known numbers except 3, 29, and 30; the small in all except 2 and 29. Style 2 (Fig. 1 *b*) occurs in numbers 27 and 29 large, and 29 small. Style 3 bird (Fig. 1 *c*) is on numbers 3, 6, 7, 25, and 30 large and 7 and 27 small. The style 4 (Fig. 1 *d*), with the cannons, is found only in numbers 1 and 2, but there are three different styles of birds, matching styles 1, 2, and 3. This tabulation I have made from an examination of all the collections I have been able to locate, amounting to possibly 400 buttons, and my own collection of 80 which includes all the numbers except 10. The tabulation may not, therefore, be complete, but if there are any other numbers they are extremely rare.

None of the disc buttons have any markings on the back, but the ball type bears the inscription "Bushby–London" encircling the shank. The Registrar of Business Names in England has no record of this firm. Since the lettering on the ball and disc types is the same style and size, it seems reasonable to assume that they were all made by the same English firm and if so it eliminates the possibility that they were made for Napoleon, a theory that is sometimes advanced (MacLennan 1953:

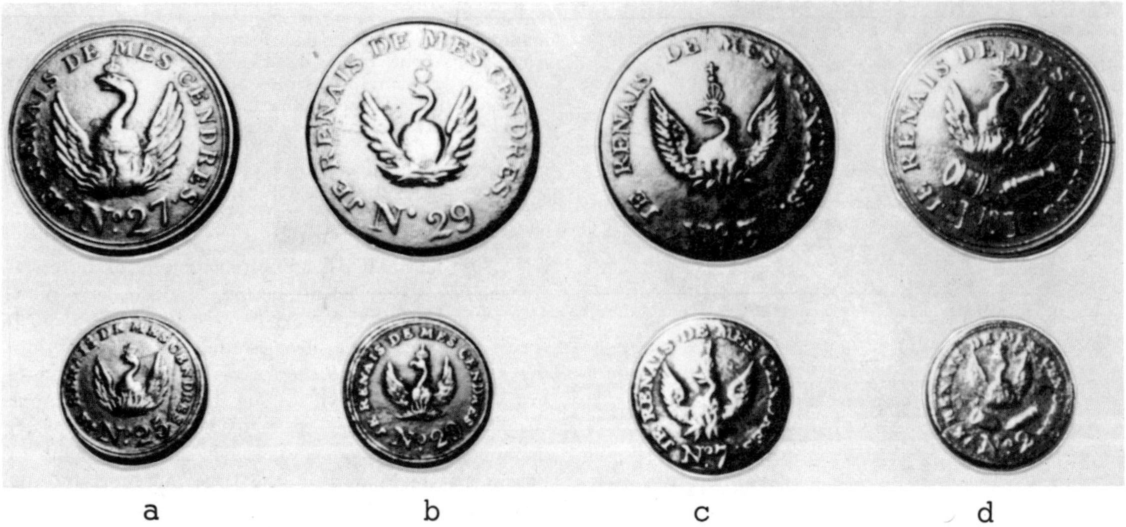

FIG. 1 [Strong]. Large and small disc types of the four styles of Phoenix buttons. *a*, style 1; *b*, style 2; *c*, style 3; *d*, style 4.

21). Furthermore, the complete catalogue of French military buttons compiled by Louis Fallou illustrates no Phoenix birds.

It has been established that the buttons were made for King Christophe of Haiti but whether they were ever delivered to him is unknown. Christophe used the Phoenix bird extensively. An old cut shows it on his crown and what appears to be a coat of arms, and it is on his officers' sword belt buckles complete with the same motto. They arrived on the Columbia River prior to 1835 because they are found in the old Multnomah village site of the Chinook Indians on Sauvies Island near Portland, Oregon, a site known to have been deserted by that date. It is known that the Hudson's Bay Company did not bring them in, and their concentrated distribution on the lower river seems to eliminate the North West Company which did extensive trading on the upper river. Because they are so abundant in the Cowlitz–Willamette–Cascades part of the Columbia this must be considered their original center of distribution. The buttons are comparatively rare on the middle Columbia only a hundred miles or so above Portland.

The late Norma G. Seaman, student of Oregon history, and Mrs. Nelly Church, button collector, after an extensive correspondence with various museums and button authorities, reached the conclusion that the buttons were originally part of the trade goods of Nathaniel Wyeth who came West in 1832 and again in 1833, intending to start a salmon packing and trading venture on the Columbia (Wyeth 1905). Prior to coming to Oregon, Wyeth shipped ice to the West Indies and could have obtained the buttons there, as he was already planning his Oregon adventure. It is recorded that he had buttons among the trinkets he used to purchase salmon. Phoenix buttons are found in the largest quantities in the favorite fishing places near his Fort William on Sauvies Island; the Cowlitz and Clackamas rivers, the falls at Oregon City, and the Cascades. These places were about as far from his packing plant as salmon could be transported in canoes without spoiling. Several hundred buttons have been found near these places; at one time 200 were found in one cache, and 26 were picked up from the clay on the river bank on Sauvies Island. They can be found on every one of the vault burial sites on the lower river; in the early days burial was by exposing in sheds or in elevated canoes on rocky points; all has of course disappeared long ago except the metal and stone. Since this area is about 100 miles from the ocean the coastal trading vessels must be eliminated as a source of the buttons.

We know that Phoenix buttons were made for Henri Christophe by an English firm in the early 1800's and were brought to the Columbia prior to 1835. Who brought them here is not known, but it was one of the independent traders and the evidence points strongly to Wyeth. Since but a small percentage of the buttons are perforated for suspension they probably were sold attached to uniform coats, one of the favorite early trade items especially if highly colored. Occasionally, a few are yet found clinging to fabric that was preserved by their copper salts.

MACLENNAN, WILLIAM

1953 Restorer of the Missions. *Westways*, Vol. 45, No. 10, pp. 20–1. Los Angeles.

WYETH, J. B.

1905 Oregon, or a Short History of a Long Journey from the Atlantic Ocean to the Region of the Pacific, by Land. . . . *Early Western Travels, 1748–1846*, edited by R. G. Thwaites, Vol. 21, pp. 20–106. Arthur H. Clark Company, Cleveland. [Originally published 1833.]

DATING EARLY PLAIN BUTTONS BY THEIR FORM

Stanley J. Olsen

MILITARY BUTTONS bearing faces with unit or branch insignia, or those having backs with makers' names, can be assigned dates with some certainty (Olsen and Campbell 1962). However, from archaeological sites are recovered many plain buttons that have distinctive patterns, particularly as to the means of attachment, and these can be given approximate dates of manufacture based on their form alone.

This brief contribution deals only with plain 18th- and 19th-century examples, having no face ornamentation or makers' names stamped on their backs. Some of these buttons, however, were worn by the regular armed forces as well as by civilians and militia, and their use will be explained in the discussion.

As a rule early buttons were plain, of cast brass, pewter, or whitemetal with wedge-shaped cast shanks (Fig. 1 *a*); others had wooden or bone backs overlapped with thin metal fronts, usually of silver (Fig. 1 *b*). In 1767 the British War Office issued an order to the effect that regimental numbers were to be placed on buttons of officers and men of other ranks. This order was not universally adopted, and some officers as well as civilians continued to wear the plain "gentlemen's" button of bone and silver. Soldiers of the Continental Army followed the same practice from about 1784.

About the time of the French and Indian War, a popular cast button was one of plain whitemetal with an iron-wire shank or eye let into a boss at the button back (Fig. 1 *c*). This same type of button was also in use by the American and British armies during the Revolution, but differed in having cast unit or branch designations on the button faces.

Spun-back buttons were used by both civilians and the military from about 1760 until the close of the Revolution. Buttons of this type (Fig. 1 *d*) were cast from whitemetal or brass and with a brass-wire eye set into a boss on the button back. The cast button was held in a chuck and spun, while a tool cut the button back to the desired thickness. A burred edge around the eye and the concentric tool marks usually identify this type. Examination of several pairs of knee-length breeches that were worn during the Revolution revealed that this style of button was used as a fastening device. They were, however, covered with the same material as the trousers.

Plain cast whitemetal buttons with a heavy eye, cast at the same time as the button, were in use from the mid-1700's until well into the 19th century (Fig. 1 *e*). Many homes of this period had button molds that could produce six or seven buttons from each pouring. The U.S. Army used this style, both plain and with official devices cast on the button face.

Among the first two-piece brass buttons were the "bullet buttons" (named for their shape) of the period of the War of 1812 (Fig. 1 *f*). They were used by the Army General Staff, dragoons, and surgeons, as well as by the militia. They were still in use after the War of 1812 by many organizations and military bands, but the more recent examples differ from the early buttons by having the makers' names added to the backs, making it an easier matter to assign dates of manufacture. Some manufacturers began the practice of putting their names on the backs about 1800, and it was generally accepted by most companies by the 1820's.

Plain brass or bronze buttons are the most difficult to date because of the long period of their use. The first of these was a plain coin-shaped disc having a simple brass eye fastened to the back (Fig. 1 *g*). There was so little surface-bearing on the button back that loss of the button due to the breaking off of the eye was common. That this was the case is attested to by the many "eyeless" buttons of this style that are recovered from early house and fort sites, with the imprint of the wire eye still visible on the soldered surface. The design to follow was logically a similar button but one with an eye having bent-over ends to give more fastening surface for the bonding metal (Fig. 1 *h*). Many of these buttons carry the words "Treble Gilt," "Extra Gilt," "Extra Quality," or similar slogans denoting the button quality, to catch the eye of the purchaser. Not uncommon was the practice of taking these plain-front buttons and at a later date (perhaps much later than that of manufacture) stamping a design on the front by the use of a split die. This latter practice can be identified by the split anvil seam that appears on the backs of these buttons (Fig. 1 *h*). These last two styles were mainly used by civilians and militia, but they were also used as Indian trade goods and by the military. When used by the regular army, they were worn inside the leather helmets as chinstrap fastenings, or inside trousers.

About the year 1830 the second major change in two-piece, stamped, brass buttons appeared (Fig. 1 *i*). This button style was well-received by all of the branches of the military as well as by civilians, and is still being manufactured today. When used by the armed forces, the domed face (which was considerably less than that found in the bullet buttons) bore stamped designs of appropriate styles for the various branches or units and, in most instances, makers' names also appeared on the reverse faces. Large quantities of these buttons were manufactured from the time of the Mexican War on through the Civil War. Plain-faced buttons were used by civilians and also issued as trade goods to the Indians. A considerable number of these have been recovered from Indian graves dating from the 1830's and 1840's.

Trouser buttons have been changed little from the time of their introduction, about the mid-1700's, except for the material used in their manufacture. Handmade bone buttons have turned up at many fort sites, and in all stages of construction. Button blanks usually have only the center hole that was used to index the turning tool, which was held in a manner similar to a carpenter's brace and bit. After the blanks were cut, the outside four holes were drilled to hold the button to the garment in the same manner as our presentday fastenings (Fig. 1 *j*). From about the time of the War of 1812 until the close of the Civil War, a plain-cast whitemetal or lead, four-hole button was commonly used on both civilians' and soldier's trousers (Fig. 1 *k*). Any fort site that has

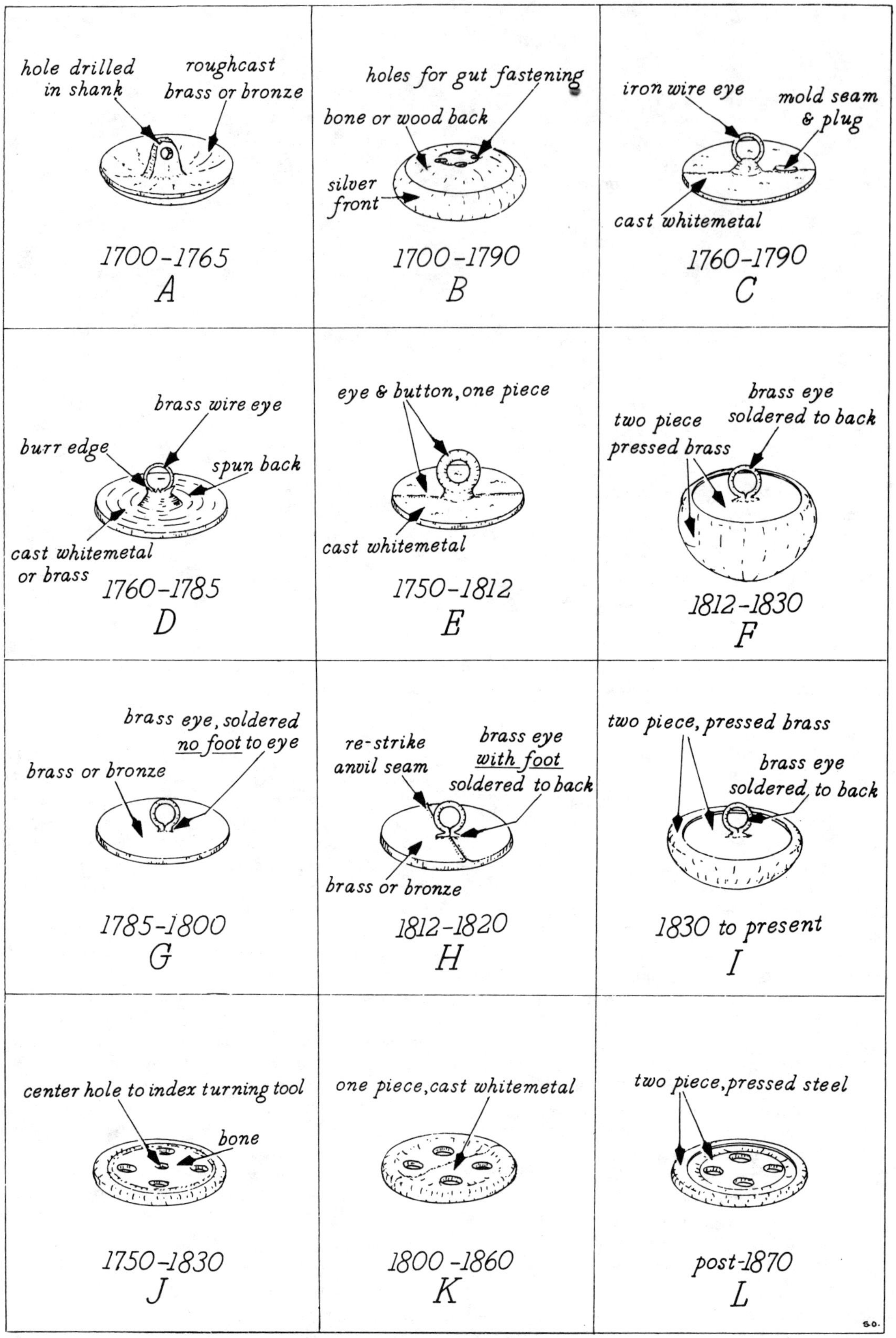
hole drilled in shank
roughcast brass or bronze
1700-1765
A
holes for gut fastening
bone or wood back
silver front
1700-1790
B
iron wire eye
mold seam & plug
cast whitemetal
1760-1790
C
brass wire eye
burr edge
spun back
cast whitemetal or brass
1760-1785
D
eye & button, one piece
cast whitemetal
1750-1812
E
brass eye soldered to back
two piece pressed brass
1812-1830
F
brass eye, soldered no foot to eye
brass or bronze
1785-1800
G
re-strike anvil seam
brass eye with foot soldered to back
brass or bronze
1812-1820
H
two piece, pressed brass
brass eye soldered to back
1830 to present
I
center hole to index turning tool
bone
1750-1830
J
one piece, cast whitemetal
1800-1860
K
two piece, pressed steel
post-1870
L
S.O.

FIG. 1. [OLSEN].

been occupied over a long span of time will have a good many button types present in the soil, as for example, Fort St. Marks, Florida (1680–1875). The last button in Fig. 1 is included because it had its beginning during the Indian wars even though it is little changed from those worn in the 20th century (Fig. 1 *l*). It is of two-piece, stamped-steel construction with four stamped holes for fastening.

When makers' names appear on the backs of these various types of buttons, or when the button fronts bear military designs, it is an easy matter to narrow down the period of use.

Much more information is needed about these early plain buttons, particularly those worn before 1750. The writer will welcome any information that pertains to archaeological finds from this period.

Acknowledgments. Sincere appreciation and thanks are extended to Col. J. D. Campbell, a noted authority on military and civilian buttons, for his valued assistance in establishing dates for many of these forms.

The courtesies extended me by Dr. Mendel Peterson in permitting me access to the collections in the U. S. National Museum of some civilian buttons taken from dated shipwrecks are deeply appreciated.

Militia uniforms having plain buttons are scattered throughout the museums of the United States. Some fine examples are preserved in the West Point Museum under the care of Col. F. Todd. A buckskin garment (collected by Lewis and Clark) with a full complement of plain buttons was examined at the Peabody Museum, Harvard University, through the courtesy of Dr. J. O. Brew. Some early buttons from a Seminole grave are in the collections of the Florida State Museum in Gainesville, Florida, and this material was generously lent by Dr. R. P. Bullen.

Olsen, S. J. and J. D. Campbell
1962 Uniform Buttons as Interpretive Aids for Military Sites. *Curator*, Vol. V, No. 4, pp. 346–52. New York.

Florida Geological Survey
Tallahassee, Florida
September, 1962

(Reprinted from American Antiquity, Volume 28 Number 4, April, 1963)

COLUMBIA RIVER TRADE BEADS

by

EMORY STRONG

Glass beads do not lend themselves very well to precise classification, description, or measurement. The varieties of color, size and shape are almost countless, and two specimens otherwise alike may be a different color, or one color may be found in several different shapes. Nevertheless, those glass beads most popular in the Indian trade do fall into several easily recognizable types, and the accompanying illustration shows those found along the Columbia River in Oregon and Washington. The rolled copper and the polychrome are not listed, being, I think, distinctive enough to be instantly recognized.

Some broad dating classification can be made from the excavations and collections I have examined, and from those I have found on old vault burial sites. Thus the type 2 is obviously the oldest of glass beads for it is found in sites where the transition from pre-contact to post-contact is apparent. It is the most plentiful type at the mouth of the Columbia, gradually being replaced by type 1 as one travels upstream. I believe it to be the "coarse blue bead" and the "Chief bead" of Lewis and Clark, and the "dark blue cut glass bead" of Swan. Type 1 is, I think, the "Canton" bead of the early traders by land for it is found in graduated sizes as listed in Company records and is most plentiful where the North West and the Hudson's Bay Companies were most active. The type 1 and type 2 combined total one third or more of all the trade beads found along the river, as estimated by the collections I have examined.

In the following description a "large hole" means large in proportion to the size of the bead and may be as much as three quarters of the diameter, as in type 2.

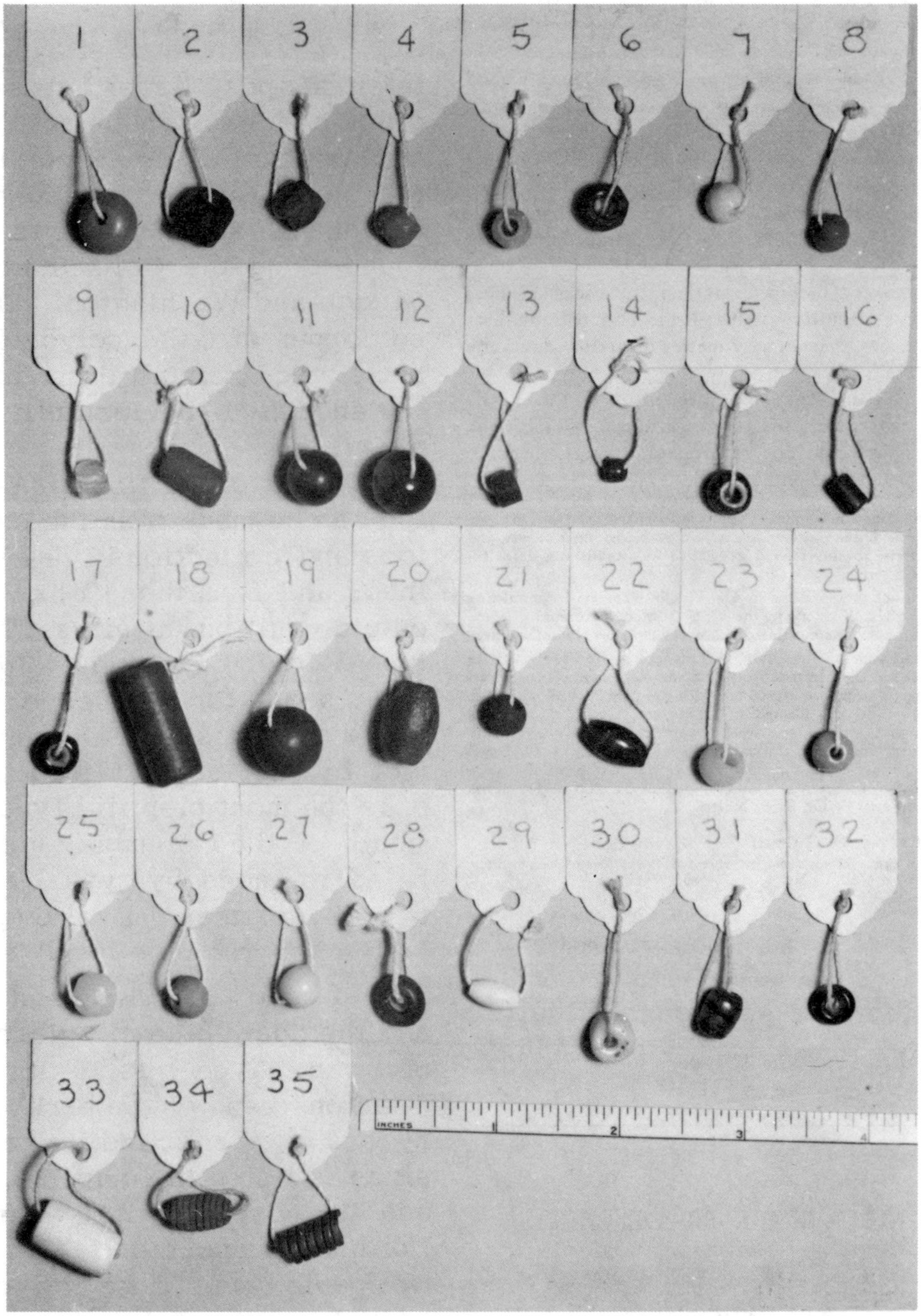

COLUMBIA RIVER TRADE BEAD TYPES

KEY TO TRADE BEAD TYPES →

1. Robin's egg blue, opaque, small hole. Various sizes from seed bead up to one half inch in diameter.

2. Blue, light to dark, translucent, faceted, large hole, various sizes from one-eighth to one-half inch in diameter. Ends rough as though broken from a tube. Often misshapen. Sometimes called "Russian" bead.

3. Light blue, translucent, faceted, fairly large hole with two concentric layers of lighter blue around it. Fairly common.

4. Light blue, faceted, opaque, large hole surrounded with concentric layer of lighter blue.

5. Very light blue, faceted, opaque, large hole surrounded by concentric layer of lighter blue.

6. Light green, faceted, translucent, large hole. Late type.

7. White, opaque, almost globular with many smooth facets, fairly small hole. Types 7, 8, 24 and 26 are similar except for color.

8. Light blue, otherwise similar to type 7.

9. Clear, faceted, tubular, large hole, rough ends like type 2.

10. Dark blue, opaque, tubular, medium hole, ends rounded. Color and texture similar to type 1.

11. Green, translucent, globular, small hole, modern. Rare.

12. Blue, beautifully translucent, globular, small hole. Comes in graduated sizes and was probably sold already strung. Sizes up to five-eighths inch diameter. Corrodes easily. Modern. Probably after 1880.

13. Dark blue, opaque, cylindrical, large hole. Modern.

14. Brick red, opaque with translucent green inner lining. Comes in many sizes, large ones rare on the Columbia. This is the Cornaline d'Allepo; see page 19. Types 15, 16, 17, 18, 19 and 20 are the later variations of this type.

15. Brick red, opaque, cylindrical, large hole surrounded by white opaque layer. Fairly rare on the Columbia.

16. Red, tubular, fairly small hole with white opaque lining.

17. Red, short barrel shape, nearly opaque, medium hole with yellow opaque lining. Easily broken.

18. Red, cylindrical, opaque, one inch or more long, medium hole with layer of yellow.

19. Red, cylindrical, opaque, small hole surrounded by yellow.

20. Red, barrel shape, small hole surrounded by yellow, common.

21. Brass shell, large hole, from late 19th and early 20th century sites. Next to rolled copper, this is the most common metal bead.

22. Red, translucent, barrel shape, small hole. Modern.

23. Very light blue, translucent, barrel shape, large hole.

24. Greenish grey, otherwise similar to type 7.

25. Milky white, translucent, faceted, small hole.

26. Blue grey, otherwise similar to type 7.

27. White, opaque, cylindrical.

28. Brown, translucent, short barrel shape, large hole.

29. White, opaque, long barrel shape, small size only.

30. White, opaque, misshapen, medium hole, obviously tumbled in a barrel while hot. Called "quartz" bead. From older sites.

31. Red with spiral pattern, slightly translucent, large hole.

32. Blue, translucent, large hole, misshapen. Not found on the Columbia. Tag on specimen reads "Hyshan, Mont." Some stone beads on specimen string.

33. White, opaque, cylindrical.

34. Round brass wire, wound.

35. Square brass wire, wound.

BIBLIOGRAPHY

1. Castillo, Bernard Diaz Del, The True History of the Conquest of New Spain , three vols., Vol. 1, Hakluyt Society Publication, Series II, Vol. XXIII, London, 1908, pp. 61-62.

2. Bowrey, Thomas A. Geographical Account of the Countries Around the Bay of Bengal, 1669-1679, Hakluyt Society, 1905, pp. 5, 9, 71, 106, 133.

3. Minutes of the Hudson's Bay Company, 1679-84, First Series, 1679-82, Vol. VIII, Hudson's Bay Record Society, pp. 316-319.

4. French Dominion, by Dunbar Rowland and A. G. Saunders, Mississippi Archives, 1701-1729, Vol. II, 1929, pp. 153-156.

5. Colonial Records of Georgia, 1738-1745, Vol. XXX, pp. 437-438, and Vol. XXVIII, Pt. 1A, p. 110.

6. Mss. Ledger of English trader at Mackinac, 1776-1777, in possession of Eric Douglas of Denver, Colo.

7. Yriarte, Charles, "Venice", translated by F. J. Sitwell, Philadelphia, 1896.

8. Kenton, Edna, The Indians of North America , 2 vols., Vol. 1, NY, 1927, p. 545.

9. Op. Cit., pp. 338-339.

10. Yriarte, pp. 363-364.

11. Op. Cit., pp. 328-329; 340; 343; 344-345.

12. Knights Mechanical Dictionary, Vol. 1, pp. 253-254.

13. For references on beads consult Godey's Lady's Book, various issues 1854, 1855, 1858 and 1859. Likewise see Whiting, Gertrude, Tools and Toys of Stitchery, Columbia University Press, N.Y., 1928, pp. 205-206.

14. Original Journals, Dodd Mead & Co., vol. VII, p. 237.

15. History of the Expedition under the Command of Captains Lewis and Clark, 3 vols. Reprint of the Biddle Edition of 1814, vol. II, Allerton Book Co., New York, 1922, pp. 342-343.

16. Shaw, Geo. C. The Chinook Jargon and How to Use It, Seattle, 1909, pp. 28 and 43.

17. McLoughlin's Fort Vancouver Letters, First Series, 1825-38. Hudson's Bay Record Society, Vol. IV, p. 41, London, 1941.

18. Cumberland and Hudson House Journals, 1775-82, Hudson's Bay Record Society, Vol. XIV, p. lxi.

19. Calendar of the American Fur Company Papers, various entries, Vol. II, Pt. I, Washington, D.C. 1945.

20. William Sturgis mss, Fur Traders in the North Pacific, Bancroft Library, Univ. of Calif.

21. Furs for the Ladies and How They Are Obtained. Godey's Lady's Book and Magazine, Feb. 1855, pp. 108-109... data obtained from a lecture delivered by William Sturgis in Boston, 1846.

22. Bolton, H.E., Palou's History of California, Vol. III, p. 190.

23. Screenings, Vol. 7, No. 2.

24. Ford, Grace H., The Button Collector's History, Springfield, Mass., 1943.

25. Wedel, Waldo R., and Griffenhagen, Geo. B., "An English Balsam Among the Dakota Aborigines". American Journal of Pharmacy, 1954. 126. 409-15. Also, Young, James Harvey, and Griffenhagen, Geo. B., "Old English Patent Medicines in America," The Chemist and Druggist, June 29, 1957, pp. 713-722.